Hello Kitty® Hello Everything!

25 Years of Fun!

written by Marie Y. Moss

HARRY N. ABRAMS, INC., PUBLISHERS

Contents

Kitty Karma

*n*othing less than an international phenomenon is the purr-fectly pretty Hello Kitty! From a simple line drawing created more than twenty-five years ago to the It Girl status she celebrates today, it is Hello Kitty's kind and caring face and stylish simplicity that make her an irresistible worldwide treasure. Not one to resist reinvention, Hello Kitty continues to captivate year by year with the turn of a head or a nod to a new wardrobe.

Each idyllic incarnation and vibrant venture sends devotees scrambling to make room for one more Kitty item among their collectibles. That task requires ingenuity (and closet space!) as Sanrio continues to offer more and more irresistible Kitty collectibles in order to please her millions of new fans as well as old pals who are rediscovering their sweet childhood friend. It is with an eye on integrity that Sanrio began in the mid-1990s to design and distribute more and more must-have Kitty collectibles—from toys and household comforts to clothing and accessories—in order to satisfy the growing worldwide demand for Hello Kitty's keepsakes. With her charming innocence and playful spirit, Hello Kitty has become the universal icon of fun and friendship.

Tale of a Kitty

Her story begins in 1974, in the faraway land of Japan, where Sanrio's first chief designer, Ikuko Shimizu, was asked to create a new kid-friendly character that could be used to decorate a child's snap coin purse. Shimizu knew that kids loved bears, dogs, and cats, and with the first two already introduced into the Sanrio family cast of characters, she put pencil to paper in search of a fabulous feline. But that's where the cat connection concludes. You see, Shimizu wanted this kitty to be kin. She wanted to create a cat that was kittenish for sure, but one that would certainly prefer a catnap to catnip. This kitty would enjoy the same hobbies as Shimizu, like eating ice cream and writing poetry. So, on November 1, 1974,

the first published Hello Kitty artwork

after a few rough sketches, Shimizu and Sanrio introduced the world to their overall-wearing, bow-adorned new family member—Hello Kitty. And who knew this tomboyish third-grader would arrive on the scene complete with cat stats? Such as the full and proper name of Kitty White (Hello Kitty is her nickname), type A blood, an official height of five apples, and a calculated weight of about three shiny apples. Other not-so-well-known Hello Kitty traits include the fact that while in the kitchen she is quite the expert cookie baker (having learned from her Mama) and that her favorite anytime snack is Mama's apple pie (occasionally served with honey vanilla ice cream topped with cookie crunch). When not in the kitchen, Hello Kitty can most often be found on the tennis court, studying grammar, playing the piano, writing poetry, planting in her tomato garden, or listening to Mama read her favorite bedtime story, *Mysterious Forest*. Her favorite clothing includes her playtime overalls, her striped dress (she wears it to parties), and her kimono, which always makes her feel graceful. Her wear-it-all-the-time

favorite accessory is her red hair bow, which she's been wearing since Mama brought her and her twin sister, Mimmy, home from the hospital. Kitty wears her ribbon on her left and Mimmy wears her ribbon on her right so that everyone can tell them apart.

Looking to visit the Hello Kitty residence? Well, the Whites' modest two-story brick home can be found on the outskirts of London (approximately twenty-five minutes by bus from the heart of the city). It is in this house that Hello Kitty lives with her

Grandpa
Anthony White

Grandma
Margaret White

Papa
George White

spectacle-wearing Papa George, who has a wonderful sense of humor and a love of reading the newspaper. The White family also includes Mama Mary, the former pianist who is rarely seen without her apron since baking apple pies is her favorite pastime. She also designs and sews all of Hello Kitty's clothing. A family friend, little Bear, also lives in the White home. Living just outside in the yard is the shy and therefore rarely seen mole named Moley.

A quick ride out to the countryside through the forest will bring you to the home of Hello Kitty's grandparents, Anthony and Margaret White. Grandpa White is a well-educated man whose hobby is painting, and when Grandma White is not honing her skills at embroidery, she's sure to be dishing up her famous pudding.

Moley

shy and reclusive

Mama

Mary White

Hello Kitty

Kitty White

Mimmy

Mimmy White

Bear

family friend

Daniel

Hello Kitty's boyfriend

Hello Kitty is also quite the social butterfly, surrounding herself with lots of friends. When it comes to boyfriends, Hello Kitty prefers the kind, sensitive type, but unfortunately the boy of her dreams, Daniel, is off on safari in Africa with his photographer papa. This long distance, letter-writing relationship is fine for now and Hello Kitty finds comfort surrounded by her friends. Her buddies include Tippy, Thomas, and Fifi. There's also Joey the mouse, Kitty's vest-wearing classmate who may just be the fastest runner in the school.

Thomas
busy as a bee

Kathy
considerate

Tippy
sweet and strong

Fifi
precocious

Jody
studious and determined

More of Hello Kitty's playmates include Tracy, the mischievous boy raccoon; Timmy and Tammy, the brother-and-sister monkey team; and boy dog Jody, who is studying to become a researcher. Rounding out Hello Kitty's social circle are Lorry the squirrel and the extremely considerate teen rabbit Kathy.

Hello Kitty's friendly neighbors include the very nice Mr. Bear at the delicious hamburger shop, Mama's friend the florist, the energetic cat who runs the bakery, the whistle-blowin' police officer, the amusement park ticket vendor who insists on wearing clothing bearing many pockets, Hello Kitty's dependable doctor whose office is in the town hospital, and the lady bear at the candy store, in her signature cap, who likes to serve up treats.

Tracy
mischievous

Timmy & Tammy
brother-and-sister team

Lorry
mysterious

Joey
athletic and patient

The Neighbors

The Police Officer

★MENU★
HOT DOGS ··· 75¢
ICE CREAM ··· 50¢
COLD DRINKS ··· 50¢

The Hamburger Shop Chef

The Doctor

BAKERY

Kathy & Her Mama

The Candy Shop Lady

Kitty Chronicles

Sanrio's motivation for creating Kitty White and her ever-evolving personality and style has always been that of developing a "forever friend" for pals all around the world. Her looks may change but Hello Kitty is always a loving and respectful girlfriend.

First Hello Kitty product

More than one million just-launched die-cut Kitty watches are sold!

1974	1975	1976	1977	1978	1979	1980

Designer Ikuko Shimizu creates the first Hello Kitty drawing.

Sanrio introduces Hello Kitty to the world on November 1, 1974.

Hello Kitty's first standing pose

Setsuko Yonekubo takes over as Kitty's second chief designer.

Yuko Yamaguchi's piano-playing Kitty is selected in a drawing contest to find Sanrio's next Hello Kitty designer. Yamaguchi continues to design Kitty today.

1981 **1982** **1983** **1984** **1985** **1986** **1987**

Photography design
is introduced.

Hello Kitty is chosen the
children's ambassador for
the United States branch
of UNICEF.

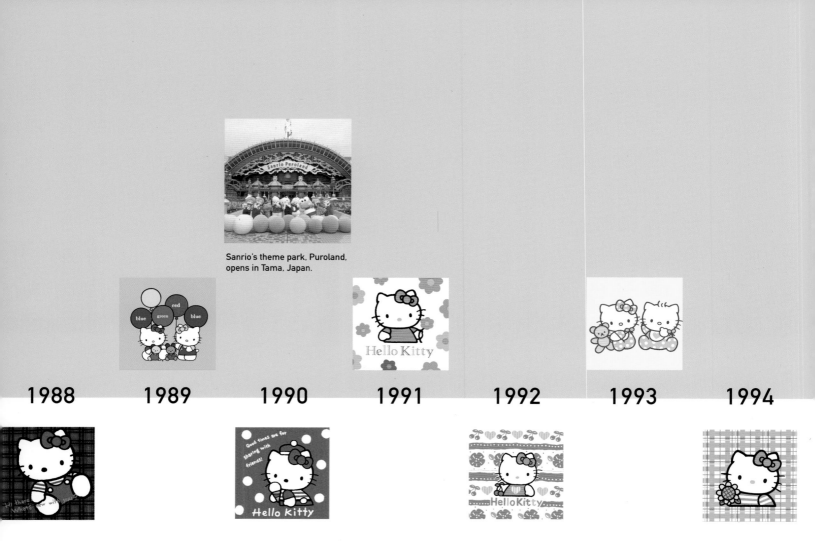

Sanrio's theme park, Puroland, opens in Tama, Japan.

1988   1989   1990   1991   1992   1993   1994

Harmonyland amusement park opens in Oita Prefecture, Kyushu, Japan.

Kitty's crush, Daniel, is introduced.

1995 **1996** **1997** **1998** **1999** **2000** **2001**

Hello Kitty Angel is introduced.

Limited edition collector's design.

Kitty Keepsakes

製造元　（株）サンリオ

This original 1975 coin purse was
the first Hello Kitty item ever!

Who could predict that a simple Kitty-adorned coin purse would launch worldwide meow mania?

One of Hello Kitty's favorite hobbies is treasure hunting. She's got quite a closetful of collectible finds. Her eye for both new items that are worth stashing away and worth-the-hunt vintage discoveries has her always keeping after her collection. Of course some treasures are rare and valuable, but Hello Kitty has discovered that the hobby of collecting is more about choosing items based on their ability to bring a bright smile to each and every friend who stops by to admire them than by their dollar value. Hello Kitty knows that collecting is a happy hobby that can last a lifetime!

What started with a coin purse spilled over into other first-time collectibles.

artist's pail 1975

vinyl purse 1975

drawers 1976

mailbox 1976

early plush Hello Kitty 1976

alarm clock 1976

letter holder 1976

canvas school bag 1976

pen 1976

chalkboard and eraser 1976

memo box 1976

learn-to-draw handkerchief 1977

Write On, Kitty!

pencil case 1976

stickers 1976

rocket crayons 1999

journal 1976

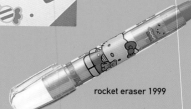

rocket eraser 1999

stamp set 1997

pencil sharpener 1999

diary 1991

date mate 2000

memo pad 2000

From pen pals to camp friends to faraway relatives, Hello Kitty's keen on correspondence. Sure an e-mail or instant message can send a quick shout-out to friends near and far, but Kitty believes it's much more exciting to stamp-and-send a handwritten letter or card. Hello Kitty knows there's nothing old-fashioned about popping a personally penned poem or note into the corner mailbox, sending it off on its cross-town or cross-country journey and into the hands of a special person. She also believes that having a stash of stationery supplies handy (from letter sets and decorated envelopes to colored pencils and whimsical stickers) can turn creative correspondence into an art form.

notebook 1999

spiral notebook 1999

Desk and school supplies have always been the heart of the Hello Kitty product line. What better way to ace a quiz or jot down notes than with her superfriendly pens, notebooks, and other fun desk supplies?

compass 1975

wooden ruler 1998

eraser set 1985

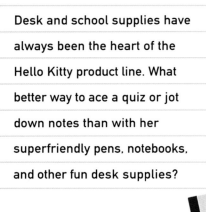

notebooks 1976

pencil case 1998

journal 1990

pencil box 1976

paper clips 1975

ruler set 1976

notepad 1992

notebook 1976

photo album 1975

pencil sharpeners 1982

memo pad 1998

stapler 1976

notepad 1976

organizer 1976

pencil sharpener 1990

color pencil set 1975

wastebasket 1991

tape dispenser 1976

crochet bag 1999

mermaid key chain 1998

Kitty à la Mode

cell phone case 1997

wool purse 1999

pearl earrings 2000

wristwatch 1999

silver ring 2000

Hello Kitty's the fashion plate who's always serving up style. From a polka-dot bikini, to a striped sailor shirt or K-adorned kimono, Hello Kitty has become one of the world's favorite fashion icons. Yes, fashion is certainly this girl's cup of tea! Hello Kitty's subtle nod to trendy timelessness keeps her up-to-the-moment modern and always smartly dressed. Over the years she has mastered the art of dressing in the styles of our times without ever overdoing it. Her fantastic fashion and accessory sensibilities reached new heights in the late 1990s when fans everywhere began scooping up her fashionista finds at a wild pace. With a greater demand for Kitty's très chic collectibles, Sanrio found itself designing more and more wardrobe-worthy items in order to keep Kitty's fans smartly styled and completely content!

pansy handbag 2000

Hello Kitty keeps it all together in totes worth noting!

vinyl tote 1985

transparent cosmetic bag 1997

canvas backpack 1991

vinyl cosmetic bag 1997

canvas bag 1989

cd case 2000

translucent tote 1999

canvas suitcase 1976

faux-fur drawstring bag 1988

felt pouch 1999

vinyl shoe bag 1990

translucent backpack 1999

fabric tote 1999

canvas bag 1976

early coin purse 1975

knitted purse 1999

wool tartan bag 1991

velvet handbag 2000

Glitzy Kitty

rhinestone ring 2000

furry cosmetic case 1999

You'd be sure to send a stylish "hello" to the twenty-first century by sporting a $30,000 (Y3,800,000), 34-diamond watch! Only 21 were created (get it?), so these limited edition clock-stoppers were collectible in an instant.

millennium edition doll 2000

You'll look so pretty in Hello Kitty!

These bags helped Hello Kitty hit the red carpet on the wrists of some of Hollywood's most famous starlets.

gingham wristwatch 1999

sequined evening bag 1999

faux-pearl clutch bag 2000

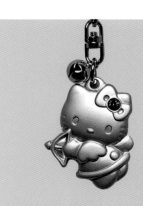

silver key chain 1998

pearl necklace 1999

key chain 1999

umbrella 1999

T-shirt 1997

swimsuit 2000

There's always room in the closet and jewelry box for Hello Kitty couture!

tank top 2001

Cool Kitty

wristwatch 1993

wristwatch 1980

T-shirt 1997

body tattoos 1997

denim bracelet 2000

socks 2000

Girly Kitty

satin purse 1999

Hello Kitty can transform just about any fabric
or bauble into a total style statement.

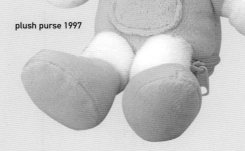

plush purse 1997

baby T-shirt 2000

pajamas 2000

quilted bags 1998

furry slippers 2000

Kitty à la Mode 33

This Hello Kitty-shaped compact contains a pretty pink toothbrush, toothpaste, and a Tiny Chum mirror, 1999.

TOOTHPASTE

Hello Beautiful

There's nothing more girly and wonderful than a well-stocked makeup case or vanity top. Hello Kitty likes to collect fun, frivolous, and functional beauty booty, especially tiny treats that fit inside her backpack, pocket, or purse. Favorites include sheer mini lip glosses, comb and mirror compacts, hair clips, and colorful cosmetic cases to keep things organized. A basket filled with grooming gear is always on hand to help keep Kitty pretty.

Hello Kitty demurely reveals a hideaway mirror on a key chain, 1999.

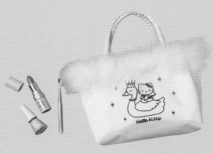

beauty kit 1999

toe separators 1999

nail polish 1999

lipstick 1997

lip gloss 2000

vanity 1999

Hey good lookin'!

curling iron 2000

footbath 1999

hairdryer 1999

hair lotion 2000

comb in case 1976

translucent mirror 1999

translucent cosmetic bag 1999

lotion dispenser 2000

toothbrush set 1996

contact lens case 2000

It's Beauty Class 101 with Hello Kitty's pamper-yourself products.

comb 1999

soap with toy 2000

translucent cosmetic bags 1999

facial tissues 1999

nail clipper 1997

kitty fresh

handkerchief 1976

perfume bottle 1999

cosmetic tote 1999

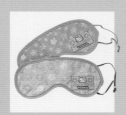

eye masks 1999

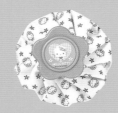

ice pack 1999

travel container set 2000

handkerchief 1976

spritzer bottles 2000

bath mitt 2000

hair scissors 2000

shower radio 2000

face towel 1978

Play with Me!

Can't a girl change her mind? Early on, Hello Kitty experimented with a variety of hair bow hues before settling on her signature red one. Always one to follow fashion, she picked a fresh flower in 1996.

When it's time for toys, Hello Kitty's collection leaves everyone envious. With a closetful of games, dollhouses, and cuddly animals, her playroom has become famous throughout the neighborhood because it is brimming with fun and filled with happiness. A play date with Hello Kitty is a sweet treat for any one of her pals, especially on a rainy day! What makes Kitty's playtime collection special? It must be her eye for the colorful, cute, and fun.

Hello Kitty's toy and game collection has grown in number over the years since these interactive playthings happen to be her favorite collectible category. Though a few special toy treats have appeared on the scene over the years, a late 1990s surge in offerings helped meet the demands of Kitty's friends and fans. This toy category continues to snowball its way into the new century, and Hello Kitty could not be more pleased with these play date perfections.

Hello Kitty computer accessory moves and lets you know when you have mail, 1999.

Hello Kitty dream house includes a swimming pool, 1999.

rocking horse Kitty bank 1976

You Make Me Plush!

early plush 1976

Traditional Japanese doll 2000

Koala Kitty 1999

Snowboard Kitty 2000

Reindeer Kitty 2000

Birthday Kitty 1999

early plush 1976

Angel Kitty 2000   **Princess Kitty 2000**   **Knitted Kitty 2000**   **Mermaid Kitty 1999**   **Bee Kitty 1999**

YEAR OF THE RAT

1996

1984

1972

1960

1948

YEAR OF THE COW

1997

1985

1973

1961

1949

YEAR OF THE DRAGON

2000

1988

1976

1964

1952

YEAR OF THE SNAKE

1989

1977

1965

1953

1941

YEAR OF THE MONKEY

1992

1980

1968

1956

1944

YEAR OF THE ROOSTER

1993

1981

1969

1957

1945

THE HELLO KITTY

YEAR OF THE TIGER

1998
1986
1974
1962
1950

YEAR OF THE RABBIT

1999
1987
1975
1963
1951

YEAR OF THE HORSE

1990
1978
1966
1954
1942

YEAR OF THE GOAT

1991
1979
1967
1955
1943

YEAR OF THE DOG

1994
1982
1970
1958
1946

YEAR OF THE PIG

1995
1983
1971
1959
1947

CHINESE CALENDAR

Hello Kitty dress-up doll 1999

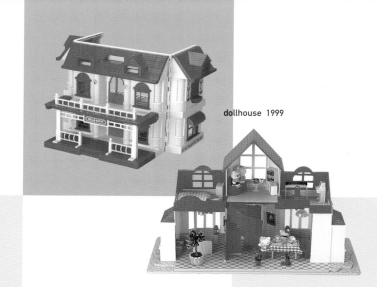

dollhouse 1999

dollhouse 1999

finger puppets 1999

doll carriage 1999

castle play set 1999

school play set 1999

rotating sushi bar 1999

mini vending machine 1999

teahouse play set 1999

Hello Kitty's Toy Box

café play set 1999

shopping cart and cash register 1999

toy boats 1999

assorted vehicles 1999

kitchen play set 1999

Toy Time

clay play set 1999

drawing set 1999

watercolor set 1999

toy airplane 1999

HELLO KITTY

musical keyboard 2000

beach ball 2000

gumball machine 1996

musical piano 1999

playing cards 2000

The Game of Life® 1999

Twister® 2000

cube puzzle 1999

Jenga® 2000

Kitty Tech

This Hello Kitty television can only be found in Hello Kitty's House at Puroland, her theme park in Tama, Japan.

calculator 1980

portable television 2000

guitar pick 1998

electric guitar 1998

Modern girls know that everything from homework to staying in touch with friends is made easier when their book bags are filled with the latest techno gadgets and gear. Hello Kitty is always eager to learn about what's new on techno turf and signs her cyber signature on the line whenever her school, or the local community center, offers classes in computers. She is also the first in line to test-drive the latest compact disc players and computer games at the friendly shop downtown and doesn't know where she'd be without her adorable portable phone.

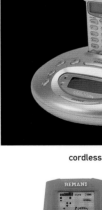

cordless phone 1999

electronic organizer 1999

solar-powered calculator 2000

disposable camera 2000

Daniel game 2000

camera 1982

electronic Japanese-English dictionary 2000

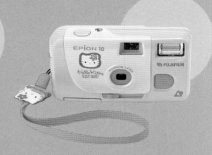

camera 1997

"Ring-Ring..."

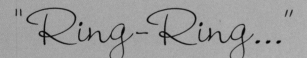

rotary phone 1981

safeguard alarm 1999

cell phone 2000

"Hello Kitty!"

phone with separate holder 2000

personal computer 2000

electronic game 1981

handheld Game Boy® 1998

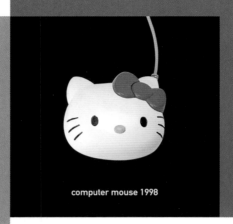

computer mouse 1998

Video and electronic games bring Hello Kitty into virtual space, 2000.

record player 1998

Kitty paw-inspired mouse 1998

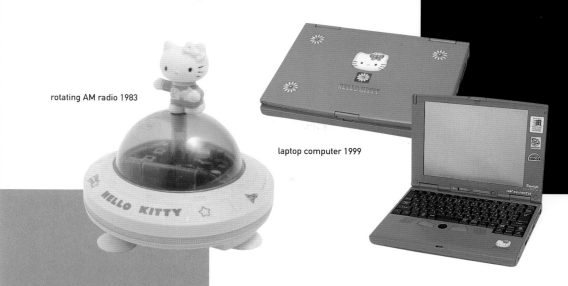

rotating AM radio 1983

laptop computer 1999

Hello Kitty shakes up digital technology with tons of irresistible techie toys.

Sega Dreamcast® 1999

boom box 1999

This Kitty Angel digital clock performs an animated water show at a preset time, 2000.

virtual pet key chain 1997

toy suitcase and travel set 1993

Vvvvrrrooooooommmmmmm!

Hello Kitty hit the road on this 1998 white Daihatsu featuring her fashionable face fifteen times. Things got locked up with Hello Kitty-shaped keys!

In 1999, Hello Kitty hit the highway again on this black Daihatsu hatchback.

suitcase 1999

Jet-Set Kitty

phone cards 1998

Out-of-doors exploring is one of Hello Kitty's favorite hobbies. Whether hiking through the forest, riding her bicycle into the next town for lunch, or traveling by plane for vacation, Kitty knows every new destination presents an incredible opportunity for learning and fun. She believes the best way to arrive in style is by bringing along both necessities and treats for the ride, all stashed away inside a favorite sturdy backpack or colorfully cool piece of luggage. Other travel must-haves include Kitty's camera, private journal, and money for snacks and souvenirs.

motor scooter 1998

bumper car 1991

backpack set 1999

Visa or Mastercard? 1998

canteen 1980

Jet-setting Kitty saw to it that her on-the-go collection included everything from a pretty pet carrier

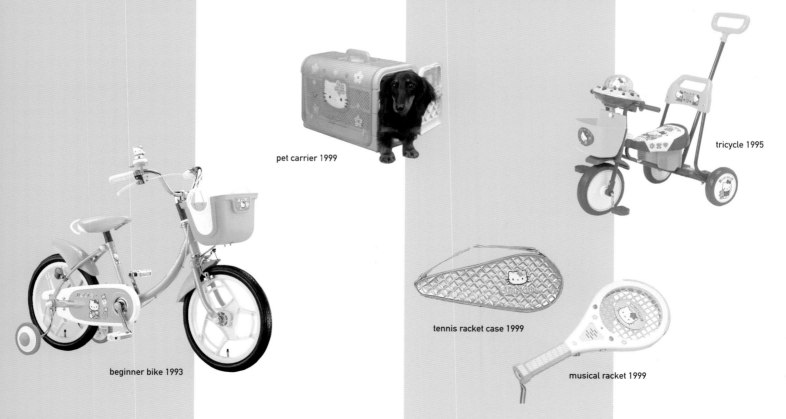

pet carrier 1999

tricycle 1995

beginner bike 1993

tennis racket case 1999

musical racket 1999

snowboards 1999

golf bag and clubs 1999

to a cool wet suit and surfboard.

wet suit and surfboard 1999

boogie board and carrying case 1999

wet suit and surfboard 1999

Kitty's House

toaster 2001

Hello Kitty's 25th Birthday tea cups 1999

coffee press 1999

clock 2001

Hello Kitty's cozy home is well stocked with creature comforts that encourage fun—cooking in the kitchen, and lots of lounging in the den. She adores decorating items that help personalize her pad. She likes to keep things neat and organized by stowing keepsakes and collectibles in colorful lunch boxes and tins, and always cleans up after herself with a push of her vacuum or a spin of her washing machine. How does Hello Kitty encourage friends to drop by on a whim? She simply arranges cozy nooks for chatting, tea parties, and homework cram sessions, and always has a decidedly delicious snack or two on hand.

casserole dish 1999

Home Girl

waffle maker 1998

oven mitt 2000

food container 2000

mini refrigerator 2000

timer 1998

flashlight 2000

True fans can create a room with a view—of Hello Kitty!

vacuum cleaner 1998

washing machine 2000

sewing machine 1999

flower fan 1999

battery tester 1983

moon cake tin 2000

chocolate 2000

candy tin 1979

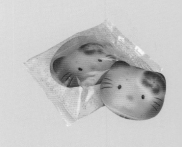

Japanese pastry 1999

toy and candy 1999

popcorn vending machine 1999

pencil case 1979

ice-cream dispenser 1999

toast 1999

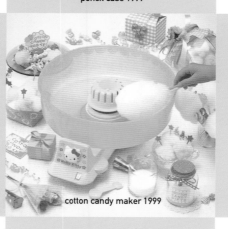

cotton candy maker 1999

toy car & candy 1999

lunch box 1976

shrimp crackers 2000

cat food 2000

macaroni 1998

sugar bowl 1976

Japanese pastry 1999

Hello Kitty's 25th Birthday rice crackers 1998

lunch box 1976

Kitty Treats

ramen cup 2000

cookie tin 1999

toy car and candy 1999

shaved ice maker 1999

milk 1997

toy and candy 1999

Japanese pastry 1999

Hello Kitty's 25th Birthday rice crackers 1998

tofu 1975

Daniel and Kitty chocolates 2001

moon cake lunch box 2000

Hello Kitty's 25th Birthday cookie 1999

Lucky couples can have a Hello Kitty-style wedding at Sanrio's Puroland in Tama, Japan.

wedding ring pillow

bridal satchel

Hello Wedding Bells

place cards and favors

wedding card

bride and groom dolls

This wedding gown design features special Hello Kitty-imprinted fabric.

Hello Kitty absolutely adores weddings! From the bride's beautiful gown and the bridal party's outfits to the toast at the reception and the couple's very first dance together, she can't think of anything more wonderful and romantic. She's been planning her very own fairy-tale wedding for as long as she can remember, dreaming of the day she herself will get to dress like a princess and walk down the aisle. Will Daniel be her lifelong mate? She's certainly planning on it (and secretly he is, too)!

champagne

crystal wine glasses

special limited edition china set

limited edition silver spoon set

sterling silver serving set

Destination Fun!

𝒲ho can resist the fun and excitement of an amusement or theme park? Not our playful pal Hello Kitty! She visits both Harmonyland and Puroland whenever she can, spending entire days (and sometimes weekends!) riding the exciting rides, enjoying the live entertainment, and browsing the shops for souvenirs. Whether celebrating the end of a school term, spring break, or just a special weekend, Hello Kitty knows she can count on both hot spots for memory-making adventures.

Puroland opened on December 7, 1990, and is located in Tama, a suburb of Tokyo. Hello Kitty is drawn to Puroland for its fun yet educational parkwide theme of "communication." She particularly enjoys the science experiment attractions and seasonal parades.

Hello Kitty also adores exploring the dreamlike Harmonyland park, which opened on April 26, 1991, in a town called Hiji in the Oita Prefecture on the Southern Japanese island of Kyushu. Local legend tells that a white bird came from the north sky to inspire the local crops to grow in abundance. Its flight is believed to be the reason for this area's farming prosperity. Hello Kitty believes that this same white bird must have landed in Oita again, bringing with it the happiness that is Harmonyland.

Hello Kitty Forever

Kitty and Mimmy mascot 1998

$\mathcal{W}$hat's ahead for this whiskered wonder girl? With an unstoppable meow-momentum, Hello Kitty's happy hidden smile is guaranteed to continue serving up surprises to old and new friends alike. She's sure to be adding adventures and accomplishments to her radiant résumé and to be sharing all of these joys and experiences with her forever friends and Kitty kinfolk.

fyi:

 Sanrio.com The official web site featuring Hello Kitty and other Sanrio characters

 Sanrio Gift Gate and Sanrio surprises The first of these Sanrio character product shops opened in Shinjuku Ward, Tokyo in 1977. The first U.S. store opened in San Jose, California in 1976.

The publisher wishes to thank everyone at Sanrio, Inc. for their help in making this project a reality. A special thanks to Bruce Giuliano, Donna Suzuki-Gilbert, Pam Bonell, and Lisa Kimura in the U.S.A. offices and Yuko Sakiyama, Mari Yakushiji, Junko Kobayashi, Riko Kogure, Keiko Minagawa, and Ryuji Arai in Japan. The publisher also wishes to acknowledge the time, talent, and overwhelming patience of Sandra Higashi and Byron Glaser.

Design by Higashi Glaser

Library of Congress Cataloging-in-Publication Data

Moss, Marie Y.

Hello Kitty hello everything! / Marie Y. Moss.
    p. cm.

ISBN 0-8109-3444-2

1. Hello Kitty (Fictitious character)—Collectibles—Catalogs. 2. Cartoon characters—Collectibles—Japan—Catalogs. I. Title.

NK1071.M68 2001
741.6—dc21
00-054833

Printed and bound in Hong Kong
10 9 8 7 6 5 4 3 2 1

ABRAMS
HARRY N. ABRAMS, INC.
100 FIFTH AVENUE
NEW YORK, N.Y. 10011
www.abramsbooks.com